MASTERS OF CEREMONY

A photo documentary of the Nazi ceremonies in celebration of Reichs Party Day Grossdeutschland at Nürnberg in 1938, and Adolf Hitler's 50th birthday celebration at Berlin in 1939.

WITH ALL PHOTO CAPTIONS IN ENGLISH AND GERMAN

Translated & edited by
Ray and Josephine Cowdery from
the two Heinrich Hoffmann books:

Parteitag Grossdeutschland
(Party Day Greater Germany)

and

Ein Volk ehrt seinen Führer
(A People Honors Their Führer)

USM, Inc.
RAPID CITY, SD USA
1998

Library of Congress Cataloging in Publication Data
USM, Inc.
International Standard Book Number (ISBN) 0-910667-38-1

Cowdery, Ray R. 1941 -
Cowdery, Josephine N. 1963 -

Title: **Masters of Ceremony**
First American Edition

1. HISTORY, Military, World War II, Nazi Party, Germany, European
2. POLITICAL SCIENCE, Nazi Party, Germany, World War II
3. PHOTOGRAPHY, Military, World War II, Nazi Party, Germany

Printed in the United States of America.

DISTRIBUTED EXCLUSIVELY
WORLDWIDE BY:

USM Incorporated
Post Office Box 2600
Rapid City, SD 57709-2600 USA
Fax: (605) 341-5488

*Notice that our address and fax number
were changed in November 1997.
Please correct your records.*

OTHER GERMAN MILITARY INTEREST BOOKS PUBLISHED BY USM, INC. INCLUDE:

Papers Please! Identity Documents of the Third Reich	ISBN 0-910667-36-5
Hitler's New German Reichschancellery in Berlin 1938-1945	ISBN 0-910667-12-8
Reinhard Heydrich: Assassination!	ISBN 0-910667-42-X
Germanische Leithefte 6-42 (Heydrich Funeral)	ISBN 0-910667-41-1
Ich Kämpfe (I Fight)	ISBN 0-910667-01-2
Hitler - The Hoffmann Photographs	ISBN 0-910667-07-1
Nazi Militaria - Fake or Real?	ISBN 0-910667-08-X
Nazi Para Military Organizations and their Badges	ISBN 0-910667-05-5
Ortsgruppe Brooklyn Yearbook	ISBN 0-910667-40-3
Dein KdF Wagen (Your Volkswagen) 1939	ISBN 0-910667-39-X
Großdeutschland	ISBN 0-910667-23-3
When The Soldiers March Through Town	ISBN 0-910667-37-3
Katyn Massacre: an Examination of the Evidence	ISBN 0-910667-43-8

Order from your favorite bookseller. If not available, write or fax USM at the address in the box above.

MASTERS of CEREMONY

PREFACE

For many years we have guided military history tours through the "Ruins of the Reich". These tours through the old *"Grossdeutschland"* were a spontaneous outgrowth of our general interest in the history of World War II, and as a result of the success of other battlefield tours we had guided for hundreds upon hundreds of Americans through Europe. The interest some people have in Adolf Hitler and the Third Reich in Germany is enormous (look in any bookstore or at the programming on TV) and crosses all lines of age, gender, politics, religion and society. We have taken passengers on our military history tours to Europe as young as 6 years old, and as old as 85. We have taken hundreds of veterans, students, professors, Christians, Jews and atheists. We have spent uncountable hours talking with these people and attempting to identify the source of their interest in the times, events and personalities of the Third Reich.

The source of many people's interest, it seems to us, is made more understandable *if one realizes* that a very large part of the population has no interest in, or awareness of the subject of World War II whatsoever. Far more than half of the people on earth today were born *after* the end of World War II. The era has predictably passed from the stage of one accompanied by the tremendous personal horror of war to an era of historical significance *for only a relatively small, specific segment* of any population. Sadly, many high school graduates today could not even tell you the years during which World War II took place. A genuine interest in any aspect of the history of World War II is very similar to an interest in some aspect of the American Civil War, the Russo-Japanese War or gold mining in the Wild West: those who care at all want to know what happened, why it happened, who was there, what equipment they used, how the participants were dressed, what they ate, etc., etc.

Speer's drawing for the lamps along the Ost=West=Achse in Berlin. These are easily seen in the photo on page 97 and in the night photo on pages 74 and 75. They are still there today, for miles along Berlin's Avenue 17 Juni.

In this respect the Heinrich Hoffmann photographs in this book are very important. Hoffmann left* an interesting and valuable resource in the two and one-half million photographs that he and his staff took before and during the Third Reich period (1933-1945) in Europe. While one person examining photographs of the parade on the occasion of Hitler's 50th birthday celebration may be drawn to the lamps Albert Speer designed to line the East-West Arterial Street, others will see the clothing and equipment of the paratroopers, while others will be attracted only to the vehicles involved. Many of the buildings wrecked by the war in Europe were later rebuilt with the aid of Hoffmann photographs, and many that were never rebuilt may be seen today *only* in Hoffmann photos.

There is a great deal to be gained and nothing at all to be lost in a careful examination of *all* aspects of any conflict, including World War II. The Hoffmann photographs in this book tell us much about the well-oiled Nazi political and military machine that dominated all of Europe for years. The expressions on the faces of Hoffmann's subjects, as well as their posture tell us more than any text could about their conviction, attitude and the degree of their success or failure.

Ray and Josephine Cowdery
Rapid City, South Dakota USA
1998

---

* The Hoffmann photographic collections were seized at the end of World War II by the US Army and are a part of the permanent collections of the US National Archives in Washington DC.

INTRODUCTION

The Nazis truly were *"masters of ceremony"*. Nobody ever did it better - not the Pope in Rome and certainly not European royalty. Traditions and ceremonies that had been practiced in Germany for centuries were responsible for a highly professionalized and deeply structured middle-class bureaucracy which the Nazis took over when they came to power by ordinary election in 1933.

Gone were the days of the "Empire" and the Second Reich, but the old imperial concept of *ceremony* was vastly expanded in Germany under the Nazis. Hundreds of new <u>ceremonial</u> <u>swords</u>, <u>daggers</u> <u>and</u> <u>medals</u> were created to be worn with scores of new <u>ceremonial</u> <u>uniforms</u> to thousands of <u>ceremonial</u> <u>events</u> in dozens of new <u>ceremonial</u> buildings; even <u>ceremonial</u> <u>castles</u>! Fortunately for history buffs, Heinrich Hoffmann and his staff of photographers were there to record the *"masters of ceremony"* at work. This book depicts two of the biggest and most elaborate ceremonial events ever staged anywhere at any time in history: Reichs Party Day Grossdeutschland in Nürnberg in 1938 and Adolf Hitler's 50th birthday anniversary in Berlin in 1939.

Hoffmann really was a very fine photographer. His ability and his National Socialist conviction came to Hitler's attention in 1919. The two became good friends and Hitler passed a lot of time in the Hoffmann Studio at number 50 Schelling Straße on the near-north side of München (Munich). The Nazi Party once had an office at the 50 Schelling Straße address and it was there in 1929 that Hitler met and courted his future wife, the photographer's assistant.

Heinrich Hoffmann was born 12 September 1885 in the town of Fürth, just outside of Nürnberg. He was trained in photography by his father and his uncle who were both well known photographers in the highest circles of German royal society. He worked under Hugo Thiele, the court photographer of the Grand Duke of Hesse in Darmstadt, for Langbein in Heidelberg and Theobald in Frankfurt aM. After moving to London he published art books in addition to his work as a photographer.

In 1910 Hoffmann returned to Germany and opened his own studio in München. He was very successful, and during the First World War he served as a photographer in the Bavarian Army. In 1919 he published his first photo book in Germany; the same year he met Hitler. Hoffmann joined the *Nationalsozialistische Deutsche Arbeiterpartei* (National Socialist German Worker Party, NSDAP or Nazi Party) in 1920, was quickly admitted to the inner circle and became a confidant of Adolf Hitler.

Upon Hitler's release from incarceration in Landsberg Prison in 1924 Hoffmann became his personal photographer. He alone was franchised to make and sell pictures of the *Führer*. By 1929 Hoffmann had opened branches in Berlin, Wien (Vienna), Frankfurt aM, Paris and Den Haag (The Hague), *and* hired a new shop assistant, a woman who was to dramatically effect his future. She was Eva Anna Paula Braun, the petite and pretty 17 year old daughter of a München school teacher.

When Hitler succeeded to the office of Reichschancellor in January 1933, Hoffmann's fortunes took another positive turn. He then published his most successful book, *Hitler, wie ihn keiner kennt (The Hitler Nobody Knows)* which made him very wealthy. It was followed over the next few years by many other books including the two from which this book was produced.

Hoffmann was a close friend of Wilhelm Ohnesorge who became Minister of the Post (Postmaster) under Hitler. With his knowledge of book and photographic royalties, Hoffmann worked with Ohnesorge to establish the system by which Hitler was paid a royalty for each time his likeness was used on a German stamp. Hoffmann's daughter Henny (Henriëtte) married Hitler Youth Leader Baldur von Schirach, which further served to weave the Hoffmann family into the fabric of upper-class Nazi society.

In 1938 Hitler appointed Hoffmann "Professor" out of respect for his craft and his artistic sense. It was Hoffmann who preselected works of art which were to be displayed at annual exhibitions at the *Haus der Deutschen Kunst* (House of German Art) in München. In 1940 Hoffmann was elected to the *Reichstag* from the district of Düsseldorf-East.

The series of photographs and books which Heinrich Hoffmann produced and sold while he was Hitler's official photographer had made him wealthy, and the most sought-after photographer of the Third Reich. The two Hoffmann books from which this volume was produced [*Parteitag Grossdeutschland (Party Day Greater Germany)* printed in 1938, and *Ein Volk ehrt seinen Führer (A People Honors Their Führer)* printed in 1939 and covering the celebration of Hitler's 50th birthday] originally sold in Germany for about 2.50 Reichs Marks (US$1.00) per copy. All Third Reich period Hoffmann books are now rare collector's items, some selling for 100 times the original 2.50 RM price.

Hoffmann was jailed by the Allies at the end of World War II and tried as a Nazi "profiteer" in 1947. The court sentenced him to 10 years in prison (later reduced to 3 years, then increased to 5 years) and confiscated nearly all of his personal fortune. He died in München on 16 December 1957. The letter H in a wreath on the title page of this book was the logo of Hoffmann Studios.

Parteitag Grossdeutschland

(Party Day Greater Germany)

This book was edited by Heinrich Hoffmann and published by *Zeitgeschichte-Verlag Wilhelm Andermann* in Berlin in October 1938 as a photo record of *Parteitag Grossdeutschland*. *Reichsparteitage* or Reichs Party Days had been annual celebrations in Nürnberg at the end of summer since the early days of the Nazi Party. The 1938 *Parteitag Grossdeutschland* was an especially important Party Day for Hitler as it was the first Party Day to be held after the annexation of the Sudetenland, Bohemia and Moravia, and the union between Germany and Austria. Germany had become *Grossdeutschland,* or Greater Germany and included populations which, although they were Germanic, had never before been a part of the Reich.

In September of 1939 Greater Germany and the Soviet Union invaded Poland precipitating war with Poland's allies, England and France, and no further *Reichsparteitage* or State Party Days were celebrated. The 1938 *Parteitag Grossdeutschland* therefore went down in history as the last, the biggest and most spectacular of all the Reichs Party Days during Hitler's Third Reich.

It may be helpful here to explain something that confuses nearly all visitors to Nürnberg who seek out the old *Reichsparteitaggelände* or Reichs Party Day Grounds: there were actually <u>two</u> areas southeast of the city which were used for the annual Nazi celebrations over the years.

<u>The first and oldest Party Day area</u> was one rebuilt in 1933 by the Nazis around a World War I memorial with its nine distinctive arches (bottom photo page 48) on the *Luitpoldhain* (Leopold's meadow). Directly across the large open field from this memorial the Nazis erected a huge limestone lectern faced with a big swastika and flanked on each side by bleachers and giant eagles (the left-end eagle may be seen in the lower photo on page 49). A great many "roll calls" were held in this *Luitpoldarena* and this is the area where most Regimental Standards were consecrated by having Hitler touch them to the "Blood Flag" (page 51).

By the mid-1930s construction was already finished on a <u>new *Reichsparteitaggelände*</u> built around the *Zeppelinwiese* just south of the old *Luitpoldarena*. The central feature of this area was the monumental *Haupttribune* (with its huge swastika in a wreath) from which Hitler often spoke. This *Haupttribune* is perfectly illustrated on pages 20, 26, 58 and 59 among others.

Only the World War I memorial remains today of the facilities the Nazis used on the *Luitpoldhain*. The bleachers, the lectern and the *Luitpoldhalle* (the photos on page 16 and 17 was taken inside it) are now gone; replaced by flowers, trees and grass. Such was not the fate of the much larger Reichs Party Day Grounds across *Bayerstraße* to the south. All of the *Zeppelinfeld* is still there as is most of the *Haupttribune* that once served as Hitler's reviewing stand.

When the Americans got to Nürnberg in 1945, they blew up the monumental wreath and swastika (page 20) that stood atop the *Haupttribune*. The Germans pretty much finished the job in 1967 by dynamiting all the columns between which long swastika banners once hung (see bottom of pages 28 and 29). The huge *Ehrenhalle* (Honor Hall) inside the *Haupttribune* is still in good condition (in spite of very poor maintenance) with its light colored limestone walls and remarkable gold mosaic ceiling of swastikas and sunbursts. It is still used at times as an exhibition hall for anti-Nazi educational displays.

The other original structure on the Reichs Party Day Grounds is the enormous *Kongressbau* or Congress Building. Begun in 1935, it was designed to replace the old *Luitpoldhalle* and other congress and meeting facilities in and around Nürnberg. When completed it was to have held 50,000 people with ease. Providing only the granite facing stone for this one building kept the concentration camp at Flossenbürg busy for years. The building was never finished. In 1942 the *Kongressbau* served as a Soviet Prisoner of War camp and at the end of the war no one knew what to do with it - a few wanted to finish it and use it for some practical purpose, but most just wanted to forget it. These days part of it is used as an automobile impound lot, while other parts of it are used to warehouse stage scenery and rolls of carpet.

The sketch-map at the bottom of the following page has been added to this book for purposes of orientation. The projected German Stadium was also begun (in 1937) but none of the superstructure was ever built. It was to have been gargantuan in every respect: almost 1800 feet long, over 1450 feet wide and over 270 feet tall, it was designed with a capacity of OVER 400,000 people!

Ankunft in Nürnberg
Arrival in Nürnberg.

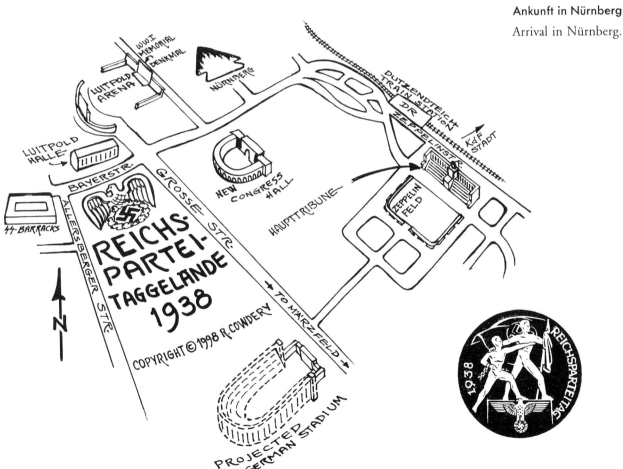

So erlebten sie Nürnberg! The Nürnberg experience!

Drive through the city.   Fahrt durch die Stadt

Greetings at City Hall.   Begrüßung im Rathaus

Empfang der Diplomaten   Reception of diplomats.

Der Stellvertreter des Führers mit Reichsleiter Rosenberg und Gauleiter Koch bei der Eröffnung der Ausstellung
The Deputy of the Führer with *Reichsleiter* Rosenberg and *Gauleiter* Koch at the opening of the exhibition.

The special performance of Lohengrin at the Opera House.   **Die Lohengrin-Festaufführung im Opernhaus**

Der Adolf-Hitler-Marsch der deutschen Jugend   The Adolf Hitler march of German youth.

14

March-past for the Führer.　　**Vorbeimarsch am Führer**

Unit flags.　　**Die Bannfahnen**

Rudolf Heß eröffnet den Kongreß   Rudolf Hess opened the Congress.

Der erste Parteikongreß Großdeutschlands   The first Party Congress of Greater Germany.

Honoring the dead.   **Totenehrung**

Reichsminister Dr. Goebbels im Gespräch mit den Nationalpreisträgern, Heinkel, Messerschmidt, Porsche, Todt
A conversation between *Reichsminister* Goebbels and National Prize winners Heinkel, Messerschmidt, Porsche and Todt.

Bei der Verkündung des Nationalpreises   At the announcement of the National Prize.

The Führer awarded the National Prize Documents.   Der Führer übergibt die Urkunden

Soldaten des Spatens   Soldiers of the Spade.

The Führer greeted laborers.　　　　　**Der Führer grüßt die Arbeitsmänner**

Der Reichsarbeitsdienst marschiert ...   The Reichs Labor Service marched ...

Feierstunde   Solemn meditation.

... before the Führer and Reichs Labor Leader.   . . . vor dem Führer und Reichsarbeitsführer

The spades were handed over to Austrians.   Spatenübergabe an die Ostmark

23

Marsch durch die Stadt   March through the city.

Naval band concert.   **Standkonzert der Marine**

Tanzvorführung   Dance presentation.

26

A picture of female gracefulness.   Ein Bild fraulicher Anmut

27

Community Day. **T a g d e r**

28

Gemeinschaft

Kraft-durch-Freude-Stadt   Strength-Through-Joy village.

National Socialist war games.   NS.-Kampfspiele

Der Fackelzug der 80 000 Politischen Leiter   Torchlight parade of 80,000 political leaders.

On the balcony of the Führer's quarters. **Auf dem Balkon des Führerquartiers**

Reichsfrauenführerin Scholz-Klink   Reichs Women's Leader Scholz-Klink.

German Women's rally.   Die Kundgebung der deutschen Frauen

Kundgebung der Politischen Leiter   Rally of political leaders.

36

The Führer saluted his political soldiers.   **Der Führer grüßt seine politischen Soldaten**

Der Lichterdom auf der Zeppelinwiese

Cathedral of Lights on the *Zeppelinwiese.*

Der Führer spricht zur Jugend   The Führer spoke to the youth.

Hitler Youth from Austria.   Hitler-Jugend aus der Ostmark

41

Der Führer bei den Schülern der Adolf-Hitler-Schulen   The Führer with pupils from Adolf Hitler Schools.

Fanfaren künden die Ankunft des Führers   Fanfare announced the arrival of the Führer.

Adolf Hitler School students.   Adolf-Hitler-Schüler

Drive through the stadium.   **Rundfahrt im Stadion**

Empfang ausländischer Jugendgruppen   Reception of foreign youth groups.

Jugend aus dem Irak   Youth of Iraq.

The Führer with the Italian youth group.   Der Führer bei der italienischen Jugendgruppe

Reichsjugendführer Baldur von Schirach mit den rumänischen Jugendführern
45   Reichs Youth Leader Baldur von Schirach with Rumanian Youth Leaders.

Generalfeldmarschall Hermann Göring spricht

General Field Marshal Hermann Göring spoke.

During the Congress.   **Im Kongreß**

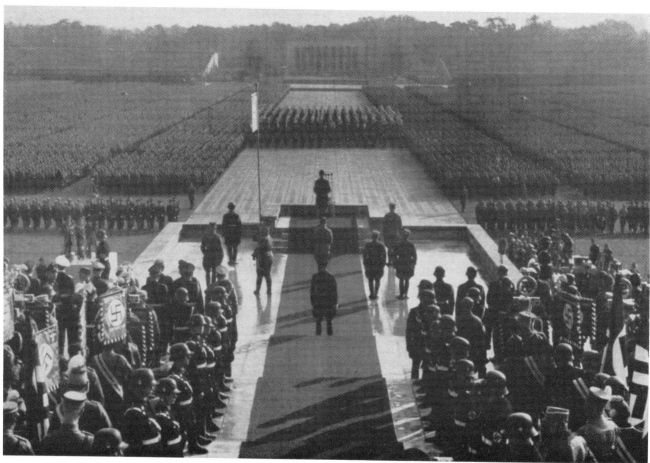

Der große Appell der SA. und ⚡⚡ im Luitpoldhain
48

The grand roll-call of the SA and SS on the *Luitpoldhain*.

Ein Volk — ein Reich — ein Führer   One people - one country - one leader.

Consecration of Standards.   **Weihe der Standarten**

51

Anmarsch zum Adolf-Hitler-Platz   March to Adolf Hitler Square.

Der erste Führer der SA. — Hermann Göring   The first leader of the SA - Hermann Göring.

52

Reichsführer-SS Himmler presents the SS-contingent to the Führer.   Reichsführer ⚡⚡ Himmler meldet dem Führer die ⚡⚡

Gauleiter Bürckel, Reichsstatthalter Seyß-Inquart und Konrad Henlein

Am Adolf-Hitler-Platz   On Adolf Hitler Square.

Marsch des braunen Heeres   March of the Brown Army.

durch die Stadt der Reichsparteitage   Through the City of the Reichs Party Day.

Day of the Armed Forces.   T a g d e r

Wehrmacht

Der Führer mit den Oberbefehlshabern des Heeres und der Kriegsmarine
The Führer with the commanders of the Army and Navy.   60

Our air defense.   **Unsere Luftabwehr**

Performance by the Armed Forces.　　　**Vorführungen der Wehrmacht**

Im Banne der Führerworte   Under the spell of the words of the Führer.

The Führer during his final great speech.   **Der Führer bei seiner großen Schlußrede**

Abschied vom Führer — Abschied von Nürnberg

66

Goodbye to the Führer - goodbye to Nürnberg.

Ein Volk ehrt seinen Führer

(A People Honors Their Führer)

This book was edited by Heinrich Hoffmann and published by *Zeitgeschichte-Verlag Wilhelm Andermann* in Berlin in May 1939 as a photo record of the huge ceremony and celebration of the 50th birthday of Adolf Hitler that took place on 19 and 20 April 1939. This "birthday party" was without equal. April 20th had been declared a national holiday so uncountable thousands of Germans filled the streets to witness a parade of over 50,000 soldiers, their horses, vehicles and weapons. Central Berlin was redecorated for the event and every available accommodation was in use by well-wishers who came from around the world for the celebration. Scores of Regiments marched through the Brandenburger Gate, down *Unter den Linden*, the *Charlottenburger Chaussee*, the *Berliner Straße* and the *Wilhelmstraße*, past the reviewing stands of the *Führer*. The streets of the entire government quarter of the German capital had been lined with monumental columns, eagles, swastikas and flags for the occasion. It was awash in the colors gold, red, white and black.

It was an event that easily equaled the regal coronations of the heads of state in European kingdoms. Gifts and flowers were showered by the ton on the *Führer* and State Chancellor, Adolf Hitler. With war less than six months away, it was the last great ceremonial event of the Third Reich. From April 1939 onward all ceremonies were smaller and centered around the deaths of heroes of the Nazi Movement such as *SS-Obergruppenführer* Reinhard Heydrich, *Generalmajor der Luftwaffe* and *SA-Obergruppenführer* Dr.-Ing. Fritz Todt and *Generalfeldmarshall* Erwin Rommel.

Some of the photographs Hoffmann and his staff shot during Hitler's 50th birthday celebration were taken in the New German Reichschancellery on *Voßstraße*, just south of the Brandenburger Gate. Examples are those pictures on pages 69, 70, 71, 78 - 81, 83 - 93, etc. The Reichschancellery was one of Berlin's newest buildings and certainly one of Europe's most impressive. Hitler had given the task of building it to architect Albert Speer in January of 1938 with the following comment: *"I have an urgent assignment for you. I will hold important conferences in the near future, and for these I will require grand halls and salons which will make an impression on people, especially on the smaller dignitaries. For the site I am placing the whole of Voßstraße at your disposal. The cost is immaterial, but it must be done very quickly and be of solid construction. How long would you need? For plans, blue prints, everything? Even a year and a half or two years would be too long. Can you be done by 10 January 1939? I want to hold the next diplomatic reception in the New Reichschancellery."*

Over 4500 workers labored in two shifts to complete the New Reichschancellery on time. Hitler followed the progress of the construction carefully and at one point commented, *"This is no longer the American tempo, it has become the German tempo. I like to think that I also accomplish more than other statesmen accomplish in the so-called democracies. I think we are following a different tempo politically and if it is possible to annex a country to the Reich in three or four days, it must be possible to erect a building in one or two years."*

The main military parade for this event moved along *Berliner Straße* and the *Charlottenburger Chaussee*, referred to in this book as *Ost=West=Achse* (East-West Arterial Street), and now called *Avenue 17.Juni*. Hitler's main reviewing stand was erected directly across the street from the *Technische Hochschule* (Technical College) at *Berliner Straße* 170-172. Parts of that building as it would have appeared *from* Hitler's reviewing stand can be seen in the photos on pages 100 - 103. The photos on pages 104 - 107 were taken *from* the *Technische Hochschule* side of *Berliner Straße* and show Hitler's reviewing stand on the north side.

Hitler had other reviewing stands for other parts of the parade. One was near the corner of the old Reichschancellery overlooking the *Wilhelmplatz* (pages 76 and 77), and another utilized Hitler's great Mercedes alongside the *Wilhelmstraße* just north of the *Wilhelmplatz* (page 82).

Hitler's car, which is seen in photos on pages 75, 82 and 97, is the fully armored Mercedes-Benz 770KW 150II which was delivered in Berlin on 15 April, just days before these photos were taken. It had a 394 horsepower 7.7 liter supercharged engine. The car consumed 10 gallons of gas and a quart of oil for every 100 kilometers (66 miles) it was driven. It weighed over 10,500 pounds empty.

The sketch-map on the following page has been added to this book for purposes of orientation.

The map below includes all the locations from which the photographs in this book of the Hitler birthday celebrations in 1939 were taken. The East West Arterial Street (Ost=West=Achse) had been rebuilt by the General Building Inspector of Berlin, Albert Speer, specifically for the occasion. Hitler had him move the *Siegessäule* (Victory Column) from its former location in front of the *Reichstag*, to the center of the traffic circle called *Große Stern* (Big Star). The proportions were not right for the *Siegessäule* to stand in the center of a huge street, so Hitler had it made taller. The column can be seen clearly at the top of the photo on page 97 as Hitler headed west on the Charlottenburger Chaussee.

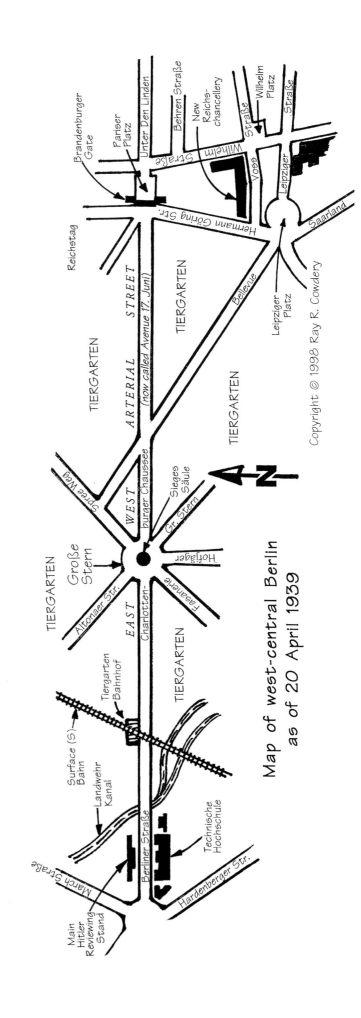

Map of west-central Berlin
as of 20 April 1939

Copyright © 1998 Ray R. Cowdery

Am Vorabend des 20. April begrüßte der Führer die beförderten SS=Junker der SS=Junkerschule Braunschweig in der Reichskanzlei

On the evening of 19 April in the Reichschancellery, the Führer greeted a group of men recently promoted in rank at the SS-Junkerschule in Braunschweig.

Die jungen Führer der SS-Verfügungstruppe gratulieren

(Left) Congratulations were given to the young leader of the militarized SS troops.

(Above) Sister Pia, the only female holder of the Blood Order, was permitted to personally congratulate the Führer.

Schwester Pia, die einzige Trägerin des Blutordens, darf dem Führer persönlich Glück wünschen

71

(Above) On the evening of 19 April, General Building Inspector Albert Speer turned over Berlin's new East-West Arterial Street to the Führer.

(Right) Hundreds of thousands of Berliners crowded the 50 meter [165 feet] wide engineering marvel [the East-West Arterial Street]. The men who helped build it, exhibit their spades.

Ein unvergänglicher Auftakt: Die Weihe der Ost-West-Achse durch den Führer
Generalbauinspektor Speer übergibt dem Führer am Vorabend des 20. Aprils die Ost-West-Achse

Hunderttausende Berliner säumen die 50 Meter breite Prunkstraße. Die Männer, die dieses Werk schufen, bildeten Spalier

Pünktlich um 21 Uhr erstrahlte die große Straße in Festbeleuchtung

At precisely 9:00 pm the festive lightning of the great street was turned on.

Adolf Hitler befährt zum ersten Male die eben freigegebene Ost-West-Achse

Adolf Hitler was the first to travel on the newly opened East-West Arterial Street.

Vor der Reichskanzlei marschierten auf dem Wilhelmplatz Regimenter der Wehrmacht auf, um dem Führer zu huldigen

(Left) Military regiments marched onto Wilhelm Square in front of the Reichschancellery to honor the Führer. (Above) After hearing the retreat, troops formed up to march past their Commander in Chief.

Nach dem Zapfenstreich formierten sich die Truppen zum Vorbeimarsch vor ihrem Obersten Befehlshaber

Im Mosaiksaal der neuen Reichskanzlei gratulierte die Führerschaft der Bewegung

(Left) The Führer congratulated the Leadership of the Movement in the Mosaic Hall in the new Reichschancellery.
(Above) Rudolf Hess spoke in the name of the first well-wishers, the Corps of Leaders of the Nazi Party.

Der erste Gratulant war das Führerkorps der Partei. In seinem Namen sprach Rudolf Heß

(Above) A delegation of Blood Order recipients offered their loyal congratulations.

(Right) Early on the morning of 20 April the men in closest proximity to the Führer offered their best wishes.

Die Abordnung der Blutordensträger entbietet in alter Treue ihre Glückwünsche

Die Männer der engsten Umgebung beglückwünschen den Führer in der ersten Morgenstunde des 20. Aprils

Am 20. April – 9 Uhr: Vorbeimarsch der Leibstandarte SS „Adolf Hitler" in der Wilhelmstraße
At 9:00 am on 20 April the *Leibstandarte SS-Adolf Hitler* marched past the Führer on Wilhelm Street.

Gratulation des Reichsprotektors Freiherrn von Neurath und des Staatspräsidenten Dr. Hacha
Congratulations from *Reichsprotektor* Baron von Neurath and [Czech] State President Dr. Hacha.

Für die Slowakei gratulierten Ministerpräsident Dr. Tiso und sein Außenminister in Gegenwart des Reichsaußenministers von Ribbentrop
Slovakian congratulations came from Prime Minister Tiso in the presence of Reichs Foreign Minister von Ribbentrop.

Adolf Hitler empfängt die Reichsregierung . . .

. . . und die Oberbefehlshaber der Wehrmacht, in deren Namen Hermann Göring sprach

(Left above) Adolf Hitler received the Reichs Leadership...
(Left below) ...and Hermann Göring spoke on behalf of the Chiefs of Staff.
(Above) Heartfelt conversation: General Field Marshal Hermann Göring delivered his sincere best wishes.

Herzliche Zwiesprache: Generalfeldmarschall Hermann Göring spricht seinen innigsten Glückwunsch aus

Mit Reichsminister Dr. Frick erschien eine Abordnung des Deutschen Gemeindetages unter Reichsleiter Fiehler und anschließend . . .

. . . überreichte Gauleiter Forster im Auftrage der Freien Stadt Danzig dem Führer den Ehrenbürgerbrief dieser urdeutschen Stadt

(Left above) A delegation of representatives of German Community Day Celebrations under *Reichsleiter* Fiehler accompanied Dr. Frick...

(Left below) ... representing the Free City of Danzig, *Gauleiter* Forster presented the Führer with a document of honorary citizenship in this incredibly German city.

(Above) The *Reichsführer-SS* and Chief of German Police Himmler and the Commander of the *Leibstandarte,* Sepp Dietrich, are shown here offering their congratulations.

Hier gratulieren der Reichsführer SS und Chef der deutschen Polizei Himmler und der Kommandeur der Leibstandarte, Sepp Dietrich

(Above) Youth groups in traditional folk costumes from all districts, made their appearance in the presence of Reichs Farmer Leader R. Walther Darré.

(Right) Best wishes from all workers were delivered by *Reichsleiter* Dr. Robert Ley.

In Gegenwart des Reichsbauernführers R. Walther Darré erschienen Trachtengruppen der Landjugend aus allen deutschen Gauen

Reichsleiter Dr. Robert Ley sprach die Glückwünsche aller Schaffenden aus

Die Ehrengabe der Auslandsdeutschen, ein Zeugnis germanischer Geschichte: die eiserne Krone der Langobarden.
Rechts der Leiter der AO., Staatssekretär Bohle.

Der Flugkapitän Hansl Baur ist mit der Besatzung der Führermaschine an diesem Ehrentage auch mit dabei

90

(Left above) Proof of Germanic history was the esteemed gift of Germans Abroad: the metal crown of Langobarden. At the right is the Leader of Germans Abroad, State Secretary Bohle.

(Left below) Flying Captain Hansl Baur and the rest of the crew of the Führer's plane were also present on this honor day.

(Above) The Armed Forces gave the Führer documentary proof of their impressive creation: a model of gigantic fortifications in the West.

Die Wehrmacht schenkt dem Führer ein Dokument seiner gewaltigen Schöpfung: ein Modell der gigantischen Westbefestigung

(Above) Happy and cheerful, the littlest ones also brought flower greetings for the Führer, and recited short verses of sweet wishes.

(Right) Uncountable pretty girls were found in a sea of beautiful colored flowers from all parts of the country.

92   Glücklich und froh bringen auch die Kleinsten dem Führer ihre Blumengrüße und sagen ihre Verslein mit lieben Wünschen

In einem farbenfrohen Blütenmeer finden sich ungezählte Sträuße, deren Blumen in allen deutschen Gauen wuchsen

(Above) As representatives of the whole of German youth, these boys and girls were lucky enough to be with the Führer himself.

(Right) The parade, a powerful demonstration of military might and determination, begins. The Führer is coming!

Als Sendboten der ganzen deutschen Jugend erlebten diese Jungen und Mädel das Glück, selbst beim Führer sein zu dürfen

Die Parade, eine gewaltige Demonstration militärischer Macht und Entschlossenheit, beginnt. Der Führer kommt!

Geschwaderflüge der stärksten Luftmacht eröffnen die große Parade der Wehrmacht am Geburtstag des Obersten Befehlshabers

(Left) Squadrons of planes of the strongest Air Force began the great Armed Forces parade on the birthday of the Commander in Chief.

(Above) The march-past of the flags and standards of all the regiments in the parade.

Der Vorbeimarsch der Fahnen und Standarten aller an der Parade teilnehmenden Regimenter

The youngest formation in our Air Force: the parachutists.

Die jüngste Formation unserer Luftwaffe: die Fallschirmjäger

Our pride - our protection: Our Armed Forces.

Unſer Stolz – unſer Schuß: Unſere Wehrmacht

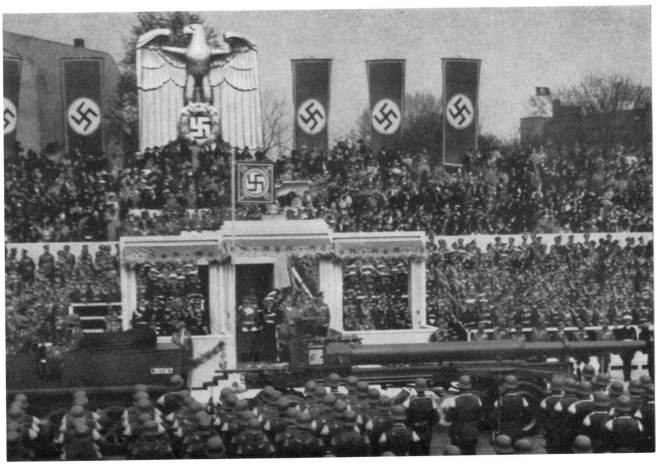

116

[Czech] State President Dr. Hacha watches the parade as guest of honor of the Führer and Chancellor.

Als Ehrengast des Führers und Reichskanzlers wohnt Staatspräsident Dr. Hacha der Parade bei

(Left) Artillery and weaponry on all military vehicles demonstrated the growth of, and the technical advancement in the equipment of the Army. Proud and amazed, hundreds of thousands of Berliners followed the grand and exciting military spectacle. (Above) Military attachés of Russia, France and England [*and* the USA] anxiously followed this unique march-past as well.

Artillerie und die Waffengattungen aller Kampfwagen demonstrieren den gewaltigen Ausbau und die Erweiterung der technischen Mittel des Heeres. Staunend und voll Stolz verfolgen Hunderttausende Berliner das spannende, großartige militärische Schauspiel. Auch die Militär-Attachées von Rußland, Frankreich und England sind gebannt von diesem einzigartigen Vorbeimarsch.

The flags were dipped in salute -

Die Fahnen senken sich zum Gruß –

- the Führer thanked his soldiers.

- der Führer dankt seinen Soldaten

Die gewaltige Truppenschau ist beendet –

The impressive review of the troops was over –

Die Truppenteile ziehen ab

- the formations of troops departed.

123

The Führer received his foreign guests of honor. $\mathfrak{Der}\ \mathfrak{F\ddot{u}hrer}\ \mathfrak{empf\ddot{a}ngt}\ \mathfrak{feine}$

ausländischen Ehrengäste